Original title:
Island Heat, Ocean Breeze

Copyright © 2025 Creative Arts Management OÜ
All rights reserved.

Author: Evan Hawthorne
ISBN HARDBACK: 978-1-80581-513-6
ISBN PAPERBACK: 978-1-80581-040-7
ISBN EBOOK: 978-1-80581-513-6

Luminescent Nights

Stars twinkle like disco lights,
Crabs tap dance on sandy nights,
Seashells gossip, oh what a sight!
Who knew the ocean had such delights?

Jellyfish glow with flashy flair,
Trying to style with jelly hair,
Fish play tag without a care,
While seagulls squawk, but few just stare.

Treasure of the Tides

Pirates search for golden dreams,
But all they find are clam-filled schemes,
Hiding treasures in seaweed streams,
   Oh, the ocean has funny themes!

Beach balls float like wayward boats,
Seagulls squawk their raucous quotes,
While sunbathers become toast,
And sunscreen turns into slippery coats!

Echoes of the Surf

Waves crash down with laughter loud,
Sea turtles swim, oh so proud,
Mermaids giggle, gather a crowd,
Sharing secrets with a splashy shroud!

Skimboards zoom by, oh what a ride,
Sandcastles lean, but they won't hide,
Seashells in pockets, they're a guide,
Each echo sings, let fun abide!

Dancing Flames

Campfire tales that make kids scream,
Ghosts and pirates, just a dream,
Hot dogs roast, they burst with steam,
As laughter bounces like a beam!

Marshmallows fly, oh what a sight,
Sticky fingers by the moonlight,
Fireflies dance, twinkling bright,
While we sing songs into the night!

Echoes of a Sun-drenched Day

The sun was hot, my drink was cold,
A seagull stole my lunch, so bold!
I chased it down, my hat askew,
The beach is fun, if you avoid the zoo.

Sandy toes and laughter loud,
Playing games with a goofy crowd!
Someone slipped, fell in the wet,
We all laughed, the best day yet.

The Warmth of Forgotten Shores

Forgot my sunscreen, oh what a mess,
Looking like a lobster, I must confess!
Swimming in water like a late-night dance,
Everyone chuckled, 'Are you wearing pants?'

A crab approached, all claws and sass,
I ran away, it had too much class!
With beach balls flying, and towels in tow,
It's just another day where sun does glow.

Cool Shadows of a Coastal Dream

The shade is nice, but don't fall asleep,
Or the seagulls will steal your fries, not cheap!
We built a castle, but waves came to fight,
It crumbled and vanished, what a sad sight!

My friend tried surfing, wiped out with a splash,
Laughing so hard, we nearly crashed!
Ice cream melted, dripped down my hand,
It's a sticky kind of fun, isn't it grand?

Awakening to Distant Horizons

I woke up late, missed the sunrise show,
Found my flip-flops, now where did they go?
The breakfast was tasty, but my hair was wild,
Thought I was a mermaid, just not that styled!

A pelican landed, tried to make a chat,
Told him my secrets, he just laughed at that!
With laughter echoing in salty air,
We danced on the sand without a care.

Heartbeats of the Coastal Wild

In flip-flops loud, they strut around,
Seagulls laugh with a squawking sound.
A crab with swagger by the shore,
Waves crash down, who needs a chore?

Sandcastles rise, then tumble down,
The king's crown lost, a frown we drown.
Shells like jewels, treasures to find,
Beach ball mishaps always unwind.

Beneath the Indigo Canopy

Palm trees sway like dancers in trance,
Sunburnt tourists at a clumsy chance.
A coconut drops, a thud on the head,
"Am I awake or just half-dead?"

Sippin' coconuts, the drinks overflow,
Is that a fish? No, just the toe!
Laughter erupts, like waves on a spree,
Who knew fun could be so fishy?

A Palette of Endless Blue

On a canvas bright, the sun paints bold,
Flip-flops and sunscreen, a life to behold.
Tanned and toasted, we dance with glee,
Till the sun's anger makes us flee.

Surfboards tumble, a comical sight,
Wipeouts create laughter, pure delight.
Cracked ice cream cones, sticky delight,
Is it melting, or just a sight?

Tranquility on a Summer's Whisper

Bare feet on sand, a lazy approach,
Fried doughnuts vanish, oh what a coach!
Kids are shrieking, in the coolness they dive,
Who needs a plan? Let's just survive!

Under the sun, we claim our turf,
With tan lines forming, we laugh and surf.
A seagull swoops in for the snacks we hold,
"Hey, that's mine!" We fight, but it's all gold.

Sapphire Horizons

Under the sun, a dance we prance,
The sand sticks tight like mismatched pants.
Seagulls squawk with witty flair,
We laugh so hard, without a care.

A coconut hat upon my head,
I trip on waves, end up in bed.
With jellyfish dreams and salty skin,
I munch on snacks while others swim.

Gentle Current's Caress

A surfboard skips, I leap and flop,
Paddle like crazy before I drop.
Palm trees sway with no order at all,
Tumbling beach balls like a bouncy ball.

The tide pulls back, I lose my hat,
Fish laugh at me, imagine that!
Sunburned noses, wild hairdos,
When the tide comes in, we can't refuse.

Radiant Dunes

Sandcastles crumbled underfoot,
A crab waves back, oh, how cute!
I bury my friends in endless sand,
They pop up surprised, isn't it grand?

Kites flying high, our laughter roars,
Surfboards stacked like ancient chores.
Chasing sunsets with a silly grin,
We toast to blunders, considering a win.

A Canvas of Blue

On the horizon, a seagull swoops,
While I'm lost in my flip-flop loops.
With icy drinks, we plot our scheme,
To catch the sun while we daydream.

With sunburnt backs and messy waves,
We chase the breeze that misbehaves.
And as the day winds down with cheer,
We dance in the twilight, hour of the beer.

Embered Horizon

The sun winks at us, wearing shades,
Laughter erupts, like ocean waves.
A crab does the cha-cha on the shore,
While seagulls plot a food heist galore.

Sandy toes tap to tropical tunes,
As we grill hot dogs under the moons.
Flipping burgers like they're flying fish,
Who knew barbecues could grant a wish?

Sweat drips down, a salty mix,
We spill our drinks in funny flicks.
A splash fight starts, we dive and dive,
In this water dance, we feel alive.

With each sip, comes a funny tale,
About how we got lost on a whale!
As the sun dives down, our shadows grow,
We laugh at the day, putting on a show.

Whispering Palm Leaves

Palm trees gossip with a leafy sway,
While I sip coconut juice all day.
The neighbor's parrot sings off-key,
Yet still, we dance like it's a jubilee.

Flip-flops squeak, a rhythm unique,
With sand between toes, we feel so chic.
The sunblock's thick, but so's our cheer,
We're stuck in paradise, and we're glad we're here.

A squirrel snatches snacks with deft precision,
While we question our life decisions.
Why wear a tan when we can burn,
In this goofy paradise, it's our turn!

As the sunset paints the sky pink,
We gather 'round, sharing a wink.
In this moment, with laughter so bright,
We wave goodbye to another hot night.

Coral Dreams

We snorkel past fish in silly shapes,
While dodging the glares of sunburned apes.
The coral giggles, tickles our toes,
In waters where the clam's got jokes to impose.

An octopus paints with vibrant hues,
While I'm caught in waves, losing my shoes.
The sound of dolphins gives us a fright,
But they just want to dance in the light.

Bikinis tangled, like a game of charades,
As we gossip about ocean escapades.
A mermaid waves, with a playful grin,
We check for scales — did we just win?

With salty hair, we sing a tune,
To the starry beat of the gentle moon.
Coral dreams and laughter combine,
In this watery world, everything's fine.

Sunlit Tides

The tide rolls in with a splashing cheer,
As we fight over who has the best suntan here.
Buckets and spades form a kingdom of sand,
While gulls plot their next meal — oh, isn't it grand?

A wave rushes in, and so does my hat,
As I dance with a fish — imagine that!
With sunburned noses and big goofy grins,
We're living it up, embracing the wins.

Ice cream drips down, what a sticky mess,
While I dodge seagulls — more than I'd guess.
Tanning fails in our slippery quest,
But laughter and fun surely is the best.

As the dusk paints orange in the sky,
We settle into stories, letting time fly.
In this playful paradise, so carefree,
We'll toast to the fun, just you and me!

Liquid Gold

A drink slips from my sweaty grasp,
It rolls away, what a funny rasp!
Chasing it down, I trip on sand,
My dignity lost to the beach's hand.

The sun shines bright, my skin's a toast,
I wave at seagulls, they think I'm a ghost.
With ice cream drips down my chin,
I wonder just where my fun began.

Flip-flops flapping, I dance in place,
Trying to keep up with the sun's embrace.
Laughter erupts with each silly slip,
While waves nearby take a tiny dip.

As evening comes, I let out a sigh,
The golden hour paints the sky.
I toast to the fun with a glass in hand,
Cheers to the antics, this crazy sand!

Horizon's Kiss

I set my chair beneath a tree,
Where the shade mingles with my glee.
The breeze plays tricks, it steals my hat,
I chase it down like it's a cat.

A crab strolls by with a little strut,
As I splash water, hear its mutt!
Jumping waves leaves my phone quite wet,
I giggle at the mess, there's no regret.

Bright towels flying, colors clash,
I attempt a dive—a most comical splash.
Fishy friends just swim away,
They've seen the dance, and it's quite the play.

The day draws to close, laughter rings,
I've battled sun and the silly things.
With toes in the sand and a drink in sight,
I dream of more laughs under starlight.

Sunbeam Dance

Fried on the sand, I'm a crispy fry,
The sun's a joker, but I still try!
To twirl and twiddle in the sun's bright glare,
Twisting around like a wacky prayer.

A beach ball soars, it bumps my nose,
With giggles surrounding, there's no time for woes.
I tumble and roll; I let out a snort,
As waves come crashing, I'm caught in retorts.

I see my shadow, it leaps with glee,
Dancing along, what a sight to see!
With sandy toes and a goofy grin,
This dance of joy, I'll try not to win.

Night falls softly, the stars peek through,
With laughter echoing, there's more to pursue.
I'll dance once more in this blissful trance,
As the moon chuckles, it joins in my dance.

Celestial Waters

I take a plunge and make a splash,
The fish around me do a dash!
They giggle too, or so it seems,
My water ballet's filled with dreams.

The waves speak secrets, oh so grand,
I try to listen, but they're all sand.
With flip-flopped feet, I make my way,
Just another joke in this ocean play.

A floating beach mat, a wild ride indeed,
I'm bobbing and weaving like a leaf in heed.
A seagull swoops, steals my snack,
I'm left to wonder, should I fight back?

As dusk draws near, I take a bow,
To the sun, the stars, the waters now.
With laughter lingering and waves so free,
I bid adieu—what a day at sea!

Drifting with the Sea's Breath

A rubber duck floats by my side,
Its quacky laugh, a joyful ride.
My sunhat's blown far to the west,
While crabs compete to be the best.

Saltwater sloshes on my feet,
Sandy toes tap to a beat.
Seagulls swoop, oh what a show!
They steal my fries, but I can't go slow.

The sun is throwing all its rays,
I've never sweated more in days.
Yet every drip, I wear with pride—
Life's a party on this tide.

With coconut drinks in hand, oh dear,
I'm starting to lose track of my beer.
But laughter's flowing like the sea,
And who needs shoes? Just let it be.

Chasing Light Across the Bay

The lanterns twitch like fireflies,
As evening wraps like a soft tie.
A crab named Larry steals my hat,
But I won't deal with that old brat!

I chase a glow that flickers bright,
While dodging waves of pure delight.
A splash, a dash, and then I see—
A dolphin winks: 'Come swim with me!'

Flip-flops flying, what a sight,
Belly flops outdo my kite in flight.
With giggles lost upon a breeze,
Tomorrow's worries, just tease, tease.

The sunset paints my silly grin,
Paint me like one of your finned kin!
As night creeps in, the stars conspire,
And now I'm just one with the choir.

Harmonies of Warmth and Wave

In the sun's embrace, all's a blur,
A seagull's stolen my last burger.
I chase it down, what a farce,
We're both performers in this circus!

The ukulele hums a tune,
While I attempt to dance a rune.
My hips don't sway, they twist and twirl,
But laughter? That's my favorite whirl!

Shells are scattered, all around,
I build a tower, then it's down!
A wave comes crashing, what a mess,
My sandcastle's now a big distress.

Yet here we are, a goofy crew,
With suntan lines and ocean stew.
Though chaos reigns, it's joy not fear,
In every laugh, warmth draws near.

Solace Under the Starlit Canopy

The stars above form quite a show,
As we roast marshmallows, watch them glow.
I try to juggle, end up in sand,
A sticky mess—what a funny brand!

A lizard spies my picnic feast,
While I declare it's time to feast!
I share a chip, now we're best buds,
This little guy's got quite the chuds.

The tiki torches sway and flicker,
While jokes go around and laughter grows thicker.
Some pun is waiting, just for me,
"Why don't crabs give to charity?"

"Because they're shellfish!" I shout with glee,
The waves join in, a jolly spree.
Under the stars, we soak it in,
Tonight, my heart is wearing a grin.

Tropical Embrace

In a land where the sun likes to tease,
Flip-flops dance, oh what a breeze!
Sunscreen battles the tan on my skin,
A coconut smile, let the laughter begin!

Sipping drinks while the seagulls snag,
My hat takes flight; oh, look at it wag!
Umbrellas twirl like they're under a spell,
The moody waves giggle, all's well that ends swell!

Flip my towel, oh what a sight,
Crabs in the sand, frolicking with delight!
Juggling seashells, I trip on a rock,
But who cares, the sun is my clock!

With friends all around, let's frolic and play,
The sun sets softly at the end of the day.
Memories made with laughter and cheer,
A toast to the warmth, let's drink up the beer!

A Dance with Sunlit Waves

The waves prance around, so cheeky and bold,
They splash at my feet, their stories unfold.
Surfboards in line, like ducks in a row,
But watch out for jellyfish doing the show!

I tried to surf, looked cool for a blink,
Then down I went with a glub and a wink.
My friends burst out laughing, what a grand fall,
I'll stick to this sand, it's comfy, after all!

Seashells aplenty, a treasure to find,
Each pocket stuffed, oh the crabs are so kind!
With sun-kissed cheeks and a grin so wide,
We danced through the foam, with the ocean as our guide.

As day turns to night, in the twilight's embrace,
We roast marshmallows with goofy grace.
Under stars that twinkle, our laughter does weave,
In this crazy chaos, who wouldn't believe?

Whispers of the Tidal Serenade

The ocean sings softly, a playful refrain,
While I sip my drink, just trying to gain
A cool bit of chill from the warmth in the air,
Watch the seagulls argue, oh such a flair!

A fish jumps and splashes, gives quite a start,
I laugh so loud, it just stole my heart.
The crabs play poker, I'm sure that they cheat,
With chips made of chips, oh what a treat!

On a floaty I drift, grabbed a bit of sun,
My laughter echoes, this life's so much fun!
I roll with the punches, outwitting the tides,
Dancing with dolphins, oh how my heart glides!

As night falls upon us, the stars twinkle bright,
We grin with the moon, oh what a sight!
With memories swirling like seaweed on sand,
I'll cherish this humor, oh isn't life grand?

Beneath the Palm's Caress

Under palm trees swaying, I settle in shade,
A hammock's my throne, I'm leisurely laid.
I munch on a pineapple, oh what a delight,
Hoping no birds steal my sweet little bite!

The breeze whispers secrets, the sun winks at me,
A coconut falls; that was close, yippee!
The laughter of friends echoes loud and clear,
As we build sand castles without a single fear!

Seagulls squawk loudly, stealing my snack,
I wave my arms wildly, give them a whack.
The tide rolls in with a giggle and splash,
Oh what a day; carefree, full of gash!

As the sun starts to set, we gather our gear,
With salty hair and hearts full of cheer.
Let's weather the storms, let's ignite the night,
With sparkles and laughter, everything's right!

Daydreams in the Sand

I tried to build a castle tall,
But ended up with a sandy wall.
Seagulls laughed, they had a show,
As I sank down, my hopes in tow.

My flip-flop flew, oh what a sight,
Chasing crabs in a primal fight.
Sunburned shoulders, can't quite tan,
I'm now the lobster, here's the plan!

A cocktail spill, what a grand splash,
A sip so sweet, then a crash!
With laughter ringing in my ears,
I'll share my woes with salty tears.

So if you come to join my spree,
Bring sunscreen, drinks, and humor, please!
Together we'll chase the goofy tide,
With giggles bright, let's take a ride.

Laughter on the Breeze

Waves are crashing with a cheer,
But I just spilled my soda here!
The gulls all hoot, they weave and sway,
While I just trip, what a display!

I tried to jog, or so I thought,
My knees gave way, I bought the plot.
A toddler passed in a tiny boat,
Said, "Hey there, buddy, get afloat!"

Sun hats bob like boats in tow,
But mine just flew, oh no, oh no!
Chasing it down in a wild parade,
I think I'll need a little aid.

With every splash, my laughter grows,
Here on the shore, anything goes!
Join my ride of slip and slide,
This silly fest, let's take it wide!

Salt-Kissed Lullaby

Under a palm, I took my rest,
Dreaming of snacks, now I'm obsessed.
A chipmunk winks with a cheeky stare,
I offered him fries, he didn't care!

My beach ball bounced, oh what a scheme,
It rolled away, right out of my dream!
The tide giggles, beckoning me,
To join the dance of the lively sea.

I thought I saw a mermaid there,
But it was just my hat in despair.
With laughter shared, the sun beats down,
A joyful swirl in this sandy town.

So let the waves sing low and bright,
In this silly place, all feels just right!
Let's hum our songs, all day, all night,
With salt-kissed joy, what a delight!

Radiant Reflections

In the mirror of the sea, I see,
A crab in swim trunks, looking free!
He winks at me, with a clumsy dance,
I crack up, oh what a chance!

The sun does flicker, like a tease,
While I lounge on, with utmost ease.
My drink's a mess, oh look! It spills,
But laughter comes, oh what thrills!

A dolphin leaps, and waves hello,
Squeaky and bright, putting on a show.
I join in, waving my arms wide,
As others stare, but I take pride!

So grab your shades, let's paint the day,
With joy and giggles, let's play away!
For nothing beats this sunny charm,
Just you, me, and nature's calm.

The Color of Twilight's Embrace

The sun melts like butter, oh what a sight,
Flip-flops are flying, everyone's in flight.
Seagulls gossip, sharing beachside lore,
Tan lines and ice cream drips down to the shore.

Dancing with shadows, a salsa in sync,
Crabs in tuxedos give us a wink.
Palm trees are swaying, it's quite the scene,
Trying to balance with a drink in between.

Life's a bit salty, like popcorn in air,
But the laughter we share, it's beyond compare.
Sun-kissed cheeks giggle under the glow,
As waves tickle toes, we steal the show.

Twilight arrives with a paintbrush in hand,
Coloring chaos across the soft sand.
Frolicking fireflies join the fun parade,
As night cloaks our antics, memories are made.

Moments in the Heat of Daydreams

Sweaty sun hats and sunglasses askew,
Beach towels are flying, make way for the crew!
Caught in a daydream, soaring so high,
Who knew a flip-flop could take to the sky?

Lemonade rivers flow down the street,
Sunbathers compete for the coolest defeat.
Tanning with dolphins, a whimsical plot,
While squirrels argue who gets the best spot.

Laughter erupts over spilled coconut milk,
Piña coladas churn through the air, smooth as silk.
A sandcastle fortress, so grand and so tall,
Crashing like waves in a comedic brawl.

Moments like these, we gather like shells,
Crafting our tales, the best of all wells.
When the sun takes a bow and the stars take cue,
We'll dance on the beach, the clowns of the zoo.

Lost in a Sea of Radiance

Floating through colors, my hat takes a dive,
With swimsuits conspiring, we're just trying to thrive.
Napping on beach chairs, lost in a maze,
While friends initiate the sunburning craze.

Surfboards sharpening, wax on and go,
Board shorts are flapping with every big show.
Mermaids conspiring to steal all our snacks,
While jellyfish giggle, avoiding all hacks.

Coconuts cracking, a fine feast or jest,
Magic horizons put our taste buds to test.
A wave of hilarity rolls into view,
As we splash in the surf like a runaway zoo.

Caught in this carnival, where fun knows no bounds,
With tides of buffoonery making us clowns.
Each sunset a masterpiece painted in cheer,
We celebrate joy, as the ocean draws near.

Surreal Days and Moonlit Nights

Under the sun's spell, our worries set sail,
With beach balls bouncing, how could we fail?
Sandy hot dogs and ketchup galore,
A slip on the mat sends us rolling ashore.

As twilight approaches, our antics take flight,
Glow sticks and laughter light up the night.
Crazy crab races, who'll take the gold?
Betting on shells, what a sight to behold!

Dancing like druids, we twirl with delight,
While the moon grins down on this wild, silly sight.
With friends all around, we'll toast with our cakes,
To the wackiest fun that our memory makes.

Surreal in this moment, we bask and we beam,
Under bright stars, we float in a dream.
With each quirky laugh, we'll forget our time,
In this comical chaos, life's purest rhyme.

Serenity's Harbor

In a hammock swinging low,
With my drink and a glow,
I spotted a crab on a roll,
Tangoing towards a hole.

A parrot squawked 'Hey, dude!',
While the tourists looked crude,
In sun hats that don't fit,
Trying hard not to quit.

A fish flipped on the line,
Mimicking dance moves divine,
As I laughed and I cheered,
At the antics I had jeered.

The sun dipped with flair,
As seagulls did dare,
To steal fries off my plate,
Now that's a twist of fate!

Dappled Sunlight

Under palm trees so tall,
I tripped and did fall,
Landed right in a pile,
Of coconuts with style.

A cat in sunglasses strolled,
With secrets yet untold,
As I stared in delight,
Wondering what's in sight.

The piña colada went spill,
I argued it was a thrill,
With tropical fish laughing,
And me, desperately crafting.

This place has a gag or two,
With sunsets that paint the view,
In the warmth, I might just stay,
And let giggles lead the way!

Rhythm of the Waves

The surfboard slipped away,
As I tried to impress Jay,
A sea turtle grinned wide,
Said, 'Wipeouts are the ride!'

With waves that dance and play,
Travelers join the fray,
Surfing to the beat,
Of a calypso retreat.

A jellyfish held a sign,
Said, 'This surf trip's divine!'
While I pondered my fate,
And the snack bar's next plate.

Caught between fish and foam,
Should I really go home?
With laughter in the tide,
This sandy joy my guide.

Tropical Reverie

On the deck, a dance unfolds,
With bizarre moves I behold,
A coconut's my partner,
As we twirl over sand, sure!

Lime wedges rolling free,
Bouncing off the spree,
Mangoes in a conga line,
Trying to sip from wine!

A crab in a tuxedo passed,
To collect laughs amassed,
While a pineapple jived away,
Setting the bar today.

As sunset paints the scene,
I sip a drink so green,
Giggling with a breeze,
In this life of funny ease!

Ocean's Blush

The sun's so bright, he wears a grin,
The crabs dance sideways, where to begin?
Seagulls squawk, their jokes are lame,
Fish flip-flop, playing the game.

Sandy toes and salty hair,
We're all applauding, without a care.
A beach ball bounces, someone might fall,
Laughing out loud, we're having a ball.

The waves tickle, they splash and tease,
A sunscreen battle, oh what a breeze!
When caught in the tide, I start to float,
My hat sails away, but I enjoy the boat.

With a coconut drink, I embrace my fate,
As the sun sets, it's getting late.
Roasting marshmallows, oh what a scene,
A night full of giggles, all sweet and serene.

Windswept Dreams

Kites soar high, catching the air,
A beach party mishap, without a care.
Sandcastles crumble, oh what a sight,
The tide comes in, they're gone in a bite.

A picnic spread, ants join the feast,
Trying to escape, oh what a beast!
Silly hats fly, tossed by the breeze,
We dart and laugh, dodging the tease.

Flip-flops flopping, a rhythmic beat,
Dancing in circles, we shuffle our feet.
With sunscreen lotion smeared on the face,
We make the worst artwork, oh what a place!

As the sun dips down, drinks in our hands,
Telling tall tales, oh isn't life grand?
With laughter around, in warmth we bask,
The night brings surprises, I'm up for the task.

Nature's Symphony

The waves crash down, in a comic tone,
Fish flopping about, protecting their throne.
A crab scuttles by, wearing a crown,
With each little step, he's dancing around.

Palm fronds sway, some join the jam,
I trip over my towel, oh here I am!
Laughter erupts as drinks go flying,
A seagull laughs too, he's not even trying.

Shells whisper tales in the beachy air,
With cada tiny secret, we sit and stare.
The sunset paints colors, a wondrous display,
While we chuckle at everything, come what may.

Of mermaids and dolphins, we create a plot,
But really, it's nature that ties our knot.
As the stars twinkle, our hearts feel free,
In this wild concert, just you and me.

Embrace of the Waves

Splashes and giggles, sunburns and laughs,
Countless flops during our crazy chaffs.
A wave comes crashing, oh what a thrill,
I lose my balance, my drink I spill!

Bikini tops fly, like flags in the breeze,
Around comes a wave, and oh, it sees!
With shouts and laughter, we dance away,
While my hat does a flip, in sheer dismay.

Tanning so bright, we shine like gold,
Check out that tan line, a story told!
Margarita spills on toes, oh what a crush,
As you see seagulls join in the rush.

When night falls down, bonfire ablaze,
S'mores in hand, we sum up the days.
With friends all around, under the stars,
Every moment's a treasure, no need for guitars.

Coral-Kissed Memories

In the sun, we dance like fish,
Chasing dreams with every swish.
Seashell hats and sandy toes,
Who needs a plan? Just see how it goes.

Laughter bubbles like the tide,
Riding waves, we take a slide.
A seagull swoops and steals my snack,
I shout, but none will take it back.

Flip-flops flying, what a sight,
Chasing crabs in pure delight.
Underwater selfies, fishy faces,
Oh, look! Another group of funny races.

Palm trees whisper, secrets shared,
While beach balls bounce without a care.
Squinty eyes and sunscreen smears,
Every moment packed with cheers!

Sunlit Footprints

On the shore, we leave our mark,
Tiny trails that fade in dark.
Giggling as we jump the waves,
A race with dogs, our hearts it saves.

With every splash, a laugh unfolds,
Tales of mischief soon retold.
Sunbaked cheeks and silly grins,
Winners celebrate with goofy spins.

Turtles surf on tops of shells,
While seagulls squawk their evening bells.
Our shadows dance, the sun bids bye,
With sand in hair, we wave goodbye.

Evenings glow with tasty treats,
S'mores and laughter fill the beats.
Let's toast to those footprints we leave,
Memories made, it's hard to believe!

Currents of Color

Diving deep in a splash of hues,
The fish are laughing, sharing views.
Polka-dots and stripes collide,
Magic swims on every tide.

My snorkel pops, what a surprise,
A crab with shades and big blue eyes.
He winks at me, then dives below,
With every splash, our friendship grows.

Rainbow reefs and silly games,
Caught in bubbles, we chant names.
With seaweed crowns, we wave and cheer,
As dolphins dance, the fun is clear.

Trading shells and sea-glass bling,
Every find makes our hearts sing.
In the depths, laughter paints the sea,
Currents swirl with glee, just you and me!

Twilight's Glow

As dusk settles, stars appear,
We roast marshmallows, never fear.
The moon's a smile, wide and bright,
Waves whisper secrets, taking flight.

Campfire songs, off-key we play,
Crickets chirp in their own way.
Laughter rings across the sands,
With each note, we take our stands.

Fireflies twinkle, dance like dreams,
Our silly antics burst at the seams.
With coconut drinks, we toast in jest,
A night like this, we're truly blessed.

As slumber calls with a gentle nudge,
We dream of adventures, never budge.
Tomorrow waits with more to explore,
With hearts so light, we'll laugh some more!

Canvas of the Sea

A canvas spread of turquoise wide,
With flip-flops slapping from side to side.
Seagulls squawk like they've lost their care,
While crabs dance around in their sandy lair.

Beachballs bounce, they fly away,
Someone's running, what a display!
Sunscreen slathered like a thick coat,
As kids float by on a wobbly boat.

Umbrellas tilt in a laughable fight,
One steals the shade, oh, what a sight!
Kites soar high, caught in a twist,
While I just sit here, sunburnt and missed.

Dolphins leap with glee in the spray,
While I juggle my snacks, what can I say?
This canvas of chaos, a colorful spree,
Keeps the laughter rolling, wild and free.

Journey to Tranquility

Setting sail with a sandwich in hand,
On waters so calm, you won't understand.
Seashells giggle, tucked in the sand,
While rubber ducks quack, quite unplanned.

A sailor's hat flies off in the breeze,
Chasing it down through palm tree leaves.
Fishy faces poke out for a peek,
While I sip coconut milk, feeling sleek.

Sunsets flicker in shades of grape,
As I try to relax but can't seem to escape.
Flip-flops float by, all lost at sea,
In this journey, it's just my snack and me.

Crabs offer me tips on how to unwind,
While mermaids giggle, dancing behind.
Laughing waves sing sweet lullabies,
In this tranquil journey, pure slapstick lies.

Turquoise Temptation

A splash of color, oh what a tease,
With lemonade dreams and a soft summer breeze.
The sun wears shades, pretending to cool,
While I drop my ice cream, what a fool!

Palm trees sway, doing the cha-cha,
While beachgoers strut like they're all stars.
Sandy toes wiggle by the shore,
As ice-water splashes an unlikely chore.

Seashells whisper tales of the deep,
While I nap on the sand, half-awake, half-asleep.
A crab scuttles by, a side-eyed glance,
While I try to join in the wave's little dance.

This tempting hue speaks of cheer and jest,
As I wear my sunhat, feeling blessed.
With laughter and fun in this playful world,
Every wave tells a story, brightly unfurled.

Tempestuous Calm

The waters are calm, or so they say,
But I've got a storm in my sunhat display.
As breezes blow with a mischievous grin,
My towel takes off, let the games begin!

Waves crash softly but tickle my toes,
As I try to keep up with where the sand goes.
Seagulls are plotting a snack attack,
While I guard my chips, not looking back.

Winds whirl around like a chaotic dance,
While I navigate through this odd circumstance.
In my cozy chair, I reign supreme,
Over salty snacks and a fun little dream.

Tempestuous? Nah, just a laugh in disguise,
As every gust brings unexpected surprise.
I'll ride this wave until the day ends,
In this calm that's wild, along with my friends.

Rhythm of the Coral Heart

The fish dance like they own the floor,
In a bubble party, what's not to adore?
Crabs doing the cha-cha, a sight quite rare,
While jellyfish float by without a care.

The seabreeze whispers secrets so sly,
As seagulls squawk, oh my, oh my!
A conch shell band plays a quirky tune,
Under the watchful, grinning moon.

Tropical drinks spill with a fizz and a splash,
While I'm trying to save my beach hat from trash.
Sandy toes tapping with joy in the air,
Who knew that sea life could lead to such flair?

So come one, come all, let's dance in the sun,
With fish and with shells, we'll have lots of fun.
In this watery world where laughter prevails,
Just watch out for waves, they tell the best tales!

Secrets Beneath the Azure

A turtle in shades, looking quite cool,
Swims by like it's some sort of pool.
The octopus winks, is he up to some tricks?
Or just showing off his eight-legged flicks?

A treasure chest filled with old, rusty spoons,
Shiny trinkets that twinkle at noon.
The fish gossip loudly, chuckling their way,
Who's dating who in the reef today?

Starfish plotting a game of charades,
While shrimp clean the stage, no need for parades.
With sea cucumbers as judges, so stoic,
It's a comical scene, almost heroic!

So dive down deep and join in the fun,
Where bubbles are laughter, and sun's never done.
Secrets of the deep, with giggles they share,
Just watch out for eels—they might give you a scare!

Serenity at the Water's Edge

Laying on towels, we snooze in the sheen,
While crabs march by, all fit and lean.
A beach ball bounces, then takes flight,
Landing on a sunbather—a comical sight!

Squirrelly seagulls steal fries from the brave,
With sneaky little plans, they misbehave.
A lifeguard snores, dreaming of fame,
As waves race in, calling his name.

Kids splash and giggle, a cacophony sweet,
While fish look on, they think it's a treat.
A clam snaps shut, it's had quite enough,
Sharing secrets of waves—oh, it's tough!

So let's sip our drinks, as the sunlight glows,
In a world of giggles, where anything goes.
Life by the shore is a whimsical blend,
Of sun, sea, and laughter that never will end!

Where Sand Meets the Horizon

Footprints in sand tell tales of delight,
As we run from the waves in a playful fright.
With shovels and buckets, kids build a mound,
While dad's lost his hat to a gust—how profound!

The sandcastle jury finds it quite grand,
But a wave's sudden justice erodes all they planned.
Seashells giggle, all shiny and bright,
As they watch the chaos, it's pure, silly sight!

Barbecues smoke, with aromas that tease,
While squirrels eye burgers with mischievous ease.
A frisbee flies high, defying all rules,
Only to land in a group of wet fools.

But oh, what a day, filled with laughter and cheer,
With sunburnt backs and cool drinks near.
As the sun sets low, painting skies with flair,
We'll toast to the moments and giggles we share!

Awash in Color

Flip-flops squeak on the sand,
As sunburned tourists take a stand.
Bright umbrellas dot the blue,
It's a circus, not a view!

Seagulls squawk with jealous eyes,
Stealing fries, oh what a surprise.
Kids are building castles tall,
While sunscreen's a sticky sprawl.

Crispy tan lines lead the way,
To a beach that's here to stay.
Laughter echoes, joy is free,
Let's play who can dive out the sea!

As sunset paints the sky in hues,
Beach ball battles break out with snooze.
Now let's capsize, don't be shy,
With a splash, we wave goodbye!

Harmony of the Tides

The waves dance in a happy jig,
While crabs are doing their own gig.
Surfboards wobbly in the fight,
Who knew sun could give such a fright?

The lifeguard's a muscle-bound sight,
Yells, 'Don't dive unless it's right!'
But kids just giggle, dive with glee,
A belly flop contest, who'll win me?

Coconuts roll like bowling balls,
While flip-flops fly at beachside stalls.
A sunburnt map across your chest,
Beats the office, it's the best!

When evening falls, the bonfire's lit,
Roasting marshmallows, oh what a hit!
Dancing shadows with songs so sweet,
A night of laughter, life's real treat!

Soothing Waters

A floatie shaped like a giant swan,
Glides through the pool from dusk till dawn.
Kids are splashing, dogs are barking,
The neighbors complain, but we keep sparking.

The sun's so bright it's making a scene,
Sunscreen smeared, what a glistening sheen.
While pool noodles drift in a race,
Splash zone champions claim first place!

Cocktails wobble on tables near,
Why sip when you can just spear?
A straw hat lifts on a breeze so slick,
Wait! Was that a dolphin, or just a trick?

As twilight falls, with giggles around,
We sing off-key, but no one's downed.
Embracing the laughter, peaceful and bright,
Under the stars, everything feels right!

Radiance at Dawn

Waking up before the sun,
Chasing light, it's so much fun.
Coffee spills and toast flies slow,
A morning ritual, on we go!

The waves whisper secrets low,
While jellyfish put on a show.
Our beach towels like banners bright,
With shrieks of joy at the first light.

Seagulls strut with pompous grace,
Scoring snacks in a bold chase.
Sand castles wobble, slowly they fall,
Tide's rising high, we're having a ball!

The day stretches, adventure calls,
From surf to sun, across these walls.
With mischief in our hearts, we play,
In a world where it's always a holiday!

Luminous Tides and Gentle Evenings

The sun wore shades, a silly sight,
Dancing dolphins under the moonlight.
Have you seen crabs in a conga line?
They pinch for joy, isn't that fine?

Coconuts fall with a thud and a bounce,
While seagulls gossip, oh how they prounce!
Flip-flops are flinging, what a big fuss,
Who knew beach days could bring such a rush?

Sandcastles crumble with a blustering breeze,
And a sunburnt tourist swats at the bees.
Laughter echoes, the night's a delight,
Under the stars, it feels so right.

The salty air tickles and makes us sneeze,
We laugh at ourselves; it's all just a tease.
As the tide pulls back, we all lose our pants,
Chased by a wave, who knew we'd dance?

Tropical Embrace

In flip-flops slipping, we take our stance,
While painted birds hold a silly dance.
A pineapple cup spills juice to the floor,
Cheers erupt with everyone wanting more!

The hammock sways, a spider may stare,
Worry about webs, or just let down your hair?
With each fruity sip, we giggle and sway,
Who knew a sunset could ruin the day?

The sun's golden glow, like butter on toast,
Makes even the palm trees seem funny the most.
We survey the beach in our wildest attire,
With glittering sunglasses, we never tire!

Here comes the wind, swirling hair in delight,
It tickles our noses, causes a fright.
But with every laugh and every crash,
We find our way home with a belly full of bash!

Sun-Kissed Shores

Oh, the sand gets hot, just like our jokes,
We build funny towers, we're laughing folks.
A crab stole my sandwich, can you believe?
He dashed with a wink; I just had to grieve!

The surfboard's wobbly, I'm feeling absurd,
Trying to rise like a clumsy bird.
With a splash and a crash, I flop with a cheer,
Even the fish laugh, I swear I can hear!

Coconut palms caper, a sight to behold,
Their leaves chatter secrets, never grow old.
A beach ball's bouncing, high and carefree,
Joining our laughter, oh what a spree!

As day turns to dusk, we gather round tight,
With goofy tales that sparkle so bright.
Under the stars, we sing a sweet tune,
As crickets provide the perfect silly swoon!

Waves of Serenity

Here comes the wave, like a furry pet,
Splat! Right in my face, but no regret.
We float like marshmallows, all cozy and fluffy,
While a nearby seagull looks quite gruffy.

The sun's a big muffin, golden and round,
We wear hats sideways, looking quite profound.
Sipping on smoothies, we're sweet as can be,
But spilled on my tongue, oh what a spree!

Fish make faces, with bubbles to blow,
Trying to out-laugh us, but they're too slow.
As crabs serve snacks, in shells oh-so-bright,
We munch on their goodies, such a silly sight!

With every rise and fall, our giggles take flight,
The tide carries humor into the night.
So here's to the laughs, the joy, and the fun,
May our beach memories shine like the sun!

Paradise Found

When the sun does rise so bright,
My sunscreen's on, but so's my fright.
I lather up with extra care,
Now I'm a greasy, shiny bear.

Flip-flops flop with every step,
I trip and fall, oh what a prep!
Sand's in places it shouldn't be,
My towel's now a sticky sea.

A crab scuttles across my toes,
He seems to know where no one goes.
I laugh and dance with crabs in tow,
But oh, they pinch – oh no, oh no!

With shades on, I join the crowd,
In laughter, we're all quite loud.
The seagulls steal my lunch anew,
So I chase them – who knew?!

Glimmering Coastlines

Surfboards glide with grace and flair,
One wipeout, and I'm flying through air!
The waves are high, my skills are low,
I'm flailing like a fish, oh no!

Sipping drinks with little umbrellas,
Chatting up those sunburnt fellas.
A parrot lands upon my head,
Now I've got a feathery spread!

Beach games start, and I am keen,
But my frisbee's more like a bean.
It hits a kid, we both just stare,
Guess I'm the jester, that's only fair.

As sunset paints the sky so fine,
The laughter mingles with the wine.
I trip again, it's all a spree,
Next year, I'll swim – or just sip tea!

Serene Drift

On a float, I dream away,
Driftwood's my throne, I'm here to stay.
But wait, what's this? A jellyfish!
A game of tag? I didn't wish!

My drink's a splash and not a sip,
I'm on a lazy, splashing trip.
The breeze whispers sweet nothings late,
But my hair looks like it's had a date!

Chasing kids who scream with glee,
And dodging all the bees, oh me!
I run, I slip, I yell with joy,
I'm now their favorite beach-time toy.

A seagull steals my hat just right,
It circles back, oh what a sight!
With laughs and splashes, we all cheer,
This day's the best, let's make it clear!

Shores of Solitude

I sought a spot, away from fuss,
Where I can sip and ride the bus.
But wait, the bus won't stop for me,
So now I'm here – just sand and sea.

The waves keep crashing, not a soul,
I talk to shells, it takes a toll.
My shadow dances with the tide,
In this odd game, I guess I glide.

A sandcastle? I tried my best,
But it looks more like a fuzzy nest.
A sand crab claims it as his throne,
I laugh at this, I'm not alone!

In solitude, I find my peace,
Though waves and critters never cease.
A funny fight, this beachy dream,
I guess solitude's a quirky scheme!

Rhapsody in Aqua

Splashes from a rogue wave, oh what fun,
Sunburned backs dance, they just can't run.
Seagulls squawk tunes, improvising some cheer,
While sunhat fashionistas boast, 'Look at me here!'

Sandcastles lean, with a questionable grace,
Frisbees collide in an aerial race.
A crab with a swagger claims sand as his own,
While beachballs bounce like they've just flown home.

Tides of Time

Watch the tide roll in, it trips on the way,
Punctuality lost, it's on holiday.
Time keeps tickling, waves hitting the shore,
As surfers complain, 'We just wanted more!'

Sunscreen fights chaos with a slippery fight,
Laughter erupts as a flip-flop takes flight.
Picnics look grand till the ants join the feast,
As friends start a dance, claiming 'You're a yeast!'

Warmth of Dusk

The sunset spills orange, a painter's delight,
While mosquitoes buzz like they own this night.
Umbrellas upside down, a chaotic retreat,
As sand clings to legs, a vacation defeat.

Glow sticks flicker in a disco mood,
While piña coladas start tasting like food.
A serenade echoes with laughter and pranks,
As evenings at shore lead to silly old shanks.

Coastal Serenade

The mermaids complain, 'We're all out of hair!'
Swimming in circles, no one seems to care.
Kites take to the sky, in a light-hearted brawl,
While clowns juggling shellfish leave everyone enthralled.

The breeze sings a tune that tickles your nose,
As snorts of a seal add to whimsical prose.
The campfire flickers, as marshmallows spark,
While crabs in the shadows rehearsal their lark.

Sun-Kissed Shores and Salty Air

On the sand, my toes do sink,
Sandwich falls, I start to think.
Flip-flops flying, what a sight,
Watch out seagulls, this is my flight!

Lemonade spills, and laughter grows,
Chasing crabs like little pros.
Umbrella's down, kaboom—what fun!
This trip's a blast, and we've just begun!

Sunscreen battles, who's the king?
Lathering up feels like a fling.
Caught a tan, but lost my pie,
Tasted great, oh, my oh my!

Evening falls with sparkler glow,
Dance on sand, watch shadows grow.
As stars peek down, I'll forever cheer,
For wild times had, with friends so dear!

The Lullaby of Warm Currents

Waves crash down like a playful shout,
Surfboards sailing, there's no doubt.
Tide pulls back with a gentle tease,
Who's chasing fish? Oh, what a breeze!

Floating on rafts, we sip our drink,
Ice cubes tumble, but not a wink.
Mermaids laugh, or so it seems,
Who knew the sea has wild dreams?

Sandy hair and a goofy grin,
Lost my hat, where to begin?
The sun caught my flip-flop feet,
Guess it's time for a feast to eat!

As dusk appears, fireflies dance,
Glow sticks fizzle—what a chance!
Tell tall tales that make us wink,
Life's a joke, just let it sink!

Vibrant Skies and Gentle Showers

Raindrops soft like a tickle fight,
Umbrellas up, what a silly sight.
Squishy puddles, boots in the air,
Splashing joy without a care!

Colors burst as storms drift past,
Rainbow's promise, oh so vast.
Dancing in the downpour's cheer,
Wet clothes make for laughter's leer!

Clouds roll away, a sunny grin,
Beach balls bouncing, let's begin.
Frisbees fly—watch where they land,
Oops! There goes my best friend's hand!

As the sun dips down again,
Sandcastle kings, who'll reign?
Chasing shadows 'til we tire,
Tomorrow brings more fun and fire!

A Mirage of Sun and Sea

A daydream's hug beneath the sun,
Chasing waves, oh, what fun!
Palm trees waving, trying to wave back,
Is that a monkey? What's with the snack?

Picnic spread, but where's the cake?
Flying ants, oh for goodness' sake!
Sandwiches served with sandy flair,
Wave hello to the quirky seagair!

Playing frisbee, then taking a dive,
Who's that swimmer? It's the beehive!
They float along trying not to drown,
While we all giggle at their frown.

As night arrives with a starry wink,
Let's roast some marshmallows and drink.
Underneath the twinkling spree,
Life's one big laugh; come join my glee!

Cascading Shadows

Sunburned skin on a beach chair,
Sipping juice without a care.
A flip-flop flies with a mighty twirl,
While crabs dance in a sandy whirl.

Coconut brains and beach toys scatter,
Daring seagulls, they squawk and chatter.
A sandcastle leaning, oh such a fright,
Its future plans were just not right.

Palm trees sway in sneaky glee,
Falling coconuts, can't they see?
A commotion when they hit the sand,
Shocked beachgoers from the grandstand.

So grab your shades and come on down,
To the place where laughter wears a crown.
With every wave, a giggle's near,
Chasing shadows, sipping cold beer.

Mango-Scented Skies

A mango pit's the ultimate prize,
Sticky fingers and sunburned thighs.
Juice dribbles down a ripe delight,
While ants plan their sticky heist tonight.

Flip-flops clash on the sunlit track,
A dolphin's showing up for a snack.
Kids splash while grown-ups just snooze,
A sunscreen battle, a comical ruse.

The hammock sways like a snarky song,
As nap-time yawns stretch oh-so-long.
A pineapple hat gets lost in the breeze,
But that's just life among the trees.

So come, enjoy the fruity affair,
With laughter echoes hanging in the air.
We'll dance with the waves till the day is done,
All sticky, sweet, and full of fun.

Glistening Seashells

Seashells glimmer, a shiny show,
Hiding critters beneath their glow.
A hermit crab with a Midwestern frown,
Plans to visit, but forgets the town.

Yo ho ho! A treasure hunt,
Digging up smiles without a front.
Each find's a giggle, a bubbling laugh,
As we quest for the perfect, comical half.

Riding waves on inflatable pools,
While seagulls caw, playing the fools.
One bird takes a dive for a chip,
Leaving beachgoers to laugh and flip.

Wellspring of fun in a scenic place,
With every shell, a silly face.
So gather 'round for a sandy spree,
As laughter echoes, wild and free.

Secret Cove Whispers

In a cove where the tide takes a peek,
Laughter rises with each playful squeak.
A treasure map drawn by a child's hand,
Leads to snacks on the soft, warm sand.

Giggling pirates in sun-kissed hats,
Swing with seaweed and dodge the chats.
With every wave, a burst of cheers,
Making memories year after year.

A mermaid sighting? Or just a friend?
Water splashes with messages to send.
Shells become phones as secrets unfold,
With stories of pirates and treasures untold.

So find your joy in this quirky plot,
Where no one cares if they burn a lot.
For in this cove of mirth and laughter,
The best treasure is the fun after.

Sunlit Journeys

Under the sun, we dance with flair,
Flip-flops flying, all without a care.
Sandy toes and silly hats,
Crabs join the rhythm, how about that?

Ice cream melting, drips down my chin,
Seagulls laugh, oh, where to begin?
With each sandy joke tossed in the air,
Our laughter echoes, pure debonair.

The sunbeams wink as they sneak away,
Coconut drinks lead us astray.
We stumble and tumble, yet stand tall,
Chasing sunsets, we'll never fall.

When day turns to night, we'll sing out loud,
With goofy grins, we'll draw a crowd.
The stars above play tag with the moon,
In this comical chaos, we find our tune.

The Language of Waves

With whispers gentle, the waves did call,
They tickle our feet and sometimes sprawl.
A fish jumps high, makes quite a scene,
As we laugh and flail, a comic routine.

A splash here, a squawk from a nearby bird,
The shuffle of sand, all absurdly stirred.
We challenge the tide, and oh, it's a race,
But it's hard when we're tripping all over the place!

The shells tell stories, oh what a tale,
Of silly seagulls with feathers so pale.
They laugh at our antics, our fruitless quests,
Creating new phrases, much like jest.

So we dance with the waves, under sun's warm gaze,
In this silly world, we'll spend our days.
With giggles and splashes, we make our decree,
The ocean's our muse, forever carefree.

Mystical Sands

Footprints lead where mischief begins,
With grandpa's hat worn sideways, grins!
The sands are hot, the stories grand,
We dig for treasure but find lost hands.

With shovels overturned, who's got the wit?
A twirl and a whirl, we're a hapless hit.
Kids building castles with moats so wide,
We pretend they're fortresses against the tide!

A sunburned back, perfect for a laugh,
While someone dodges a rogue little wave's swath.
A mighty splash, then yelling in glee,
As the tide rolls in for a playful spree.

At sunset's glow, we share tales and dreams,
The sand our canvas, or so it seems.
Our laughter resonates, oh what a dance,
In the mystical sands, we take our chance!

Breeze-Borne Secrets

A whispering breeze gave us a push,
Carried our secrets with a giggly hush.
The kites soared high, in glorious flight,
Making the clouds giggle, what a sight!

We chase tumbleweed, with ridiculous grace,
As grasshoppers join in the warm embrace.
With sandals flipped, the race is on,
Who knew such silliness could be this fun?

The palm trees sway, they shake with delight,
As we play tag under the soft twilight.
Our voices travel on that playful breeze,
With laughter echoing through the palm trees.

In this joyous chaos, we strut about,
Sharing those secrets, without a doubt.
With each chuckle, as the sun descends,
The world's a stage—oh, how it transcends!

www.ingramcontent.com/pod-product-compliance
Lightning Source LLC
Chambersburg PA
CBHW072119070526
44585CB00016B/1502